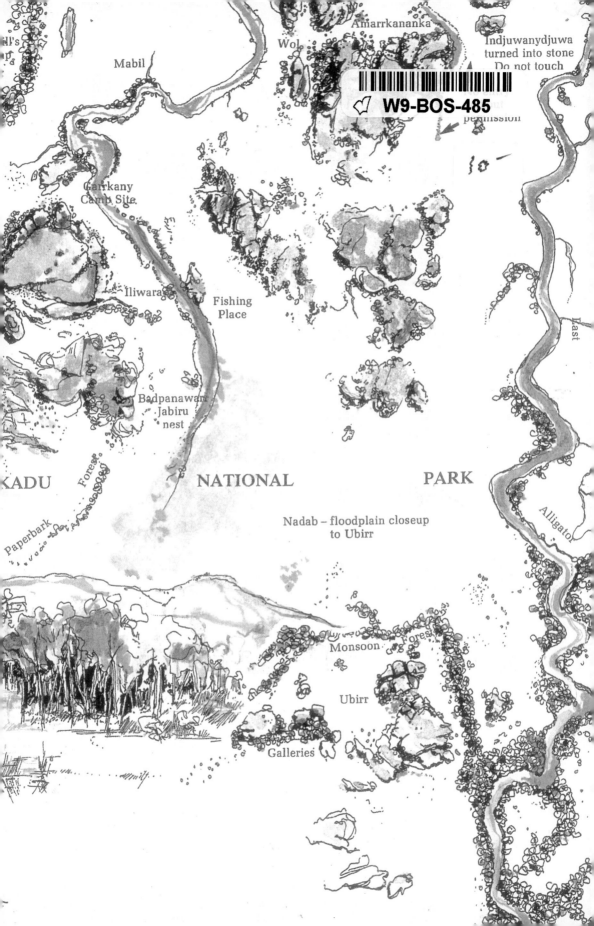

Mabil

Wol

Amarrkananka

Indjuwanydjuwa
turned into stone
Do not touch

permission

Garrkany
Camp Site

Iliwara

Fishing
Place

East

Badpanawan
Jabiru
nest

KADU

Forest

NATIONAL

PARK

Paperbark

Nadab – floodplain closeup
to Ubirr

Alligator

Monsoon   Forest

Ubirr

Galleries

I would like to give special thanks to all those who spent their time with my father and helped him tell his story,

to Stephen Davis and Allan Fox who contributed their texts from the previous editions of this book,

particular thanks to Stephen Davis for the many hours he spent with Bill transcribing the poems,

to Ian Morris, Greg Miles and Mark Lang who took the photographs,

and Jane Moore and Mark Lang who put it all together.

There is a good story within these pages.

Please read it well and learn from the wisdom within.

Jonathan Nadji, 2001
Son

Bunitj Clan
Kakadu National Park

I give you this story.
this proper, true story.
People can listen.
I'm telling this while you've got time,
time for you to make something,
you know,
history
book.

Gagudju Man
BILL NEIDJIE

The environmental and spiritual philosophy of
a senior traditional owner
Kakadu National Park, Northern Territory, Australia

 JB Books Australia

Bill Neidjie – Gagudju Man, published in 2005 by:

J B Books
PO Box 118
Marleston SA 5033
Phone +61 8 8351 1688 Fax +61 8 8351 1699.
This hardback edition published in 2005

Words	*Bill Neidjie*
Foreword	*Ian Morris*
Commentary	*Stephen Davis, Allan Fox*
Photography	*Ian Morris, Greg Miles, Mark Lang, Ted Ryko*
Design, layout, editing	*Jane Moore, Mark Lang*
Artwork	*Jane Moore*
Proof reading	*Penelope Charlesworth*
Printer	*Produced by Phoenix Offset, Hong Kong*

Photography

Mark Lang   cover, panorama below and previous page;
panoramas on pages 2-3, 4-5, 70-71, 72-73, 74-75, 78-79, 82-38

Greg Miles   pages 8, 58, 59, 60 (bottom), 62, 64 (turtles & goose), 68, 76-77, 80-81, back cover.

Ian Morris   introductory portrait of Bill Neidjie,
pages 6, 7, 12, 60 (top), 64 (lower left), 66

Ted Ryko   page 10 [courtesy Northern Territory Library Service]

FOREWORD

BILL NEIDJIE IS UNIQUE among the Aboriginal people of Australia for a variety of profound reasons.

Firstly, he belongs to a long line of people who have managed one of the most beautiful and ecologically diverse regions remaining in Australia. His land now forms one of the jewels in the crown of the world renowned Kakadu National Park. Far sighted and wise, he follows his father, Ngadambala, who played a major role in assisting the first western enterprise on this landscape – buffalo shooting and the sale of hides.

Secondly, again following in his father's footsteps, Bill has had to continue the process of carefully teaching the ever-increasing number of non-Aboriginal people who wish to share the riches of his land. He belongs to two very different worlds. To this end, he is seen as something of a 'guru' to both sides.

Thirdly, Bill has found himself as the essential negotiator in the future of his father's land – the Bunitj Clan Estate. This responsibility is combined with the knowledge that he cannot prevent these changes. Outside pressures have constantly pushed him to take some part in altering the natural and cultural landscape which has nurtured his people over one of the longest periods of human history.

His land has seen significant natural changes over time – changes in the earth's surface, sea level, climate, vegetation and animal life, as well as fluctuations in human population. These events have gradually moulded the landscape into the richness we now call Kakadu. Bill's people have observed and recorded many of these changes in the story of their land – the story of their people.

And he knows that his generation has seen the greatest social and environmental changes over that entire period. This element of tragedy is always in the background of Bill's presence.

More so than his parents, his children and his grandchildren, he has witnessed the rapid demise of his people's way of life, their recorded history, their language, their personal cultural knowledge – in effect, their understanding of themselves.

Bill did something that was foreign to his forefathers. He went to the little mission school at Oenpelli, across the East Alligator River, opposite Bunitj land. He claims that he was a poor student and did not last very long before heading for the bush again. Over the years he has watched schools in Aboriginal communities replacing the traditional learning pathways of his people, even though he has tried hard to

teach his children and grandchildren the ways of old. In his long lifetime he has watched this knowledge fade in importance to the younger generations as the ways of the world crowd in. At the same time, most of his friends and traditional associates have passed on, leaving him culturally isolated. In his old age he has had to face a vastly altered future, the sad legacy of all elderly Aboriginal people in today's world.

Nevertheless, Bill is an optimist. He can brush away sadness with his infectious laugh. Despite the limitations of poor health, Bill likes nothing better than telling stories or sharing his philosophies on the relationship between humans and the land. Many visitors to Kakadu National Park have had their experiences greatly enriched by meeting Big Bill Neidjie – Gagudju Man.

I count it as a privilege to have known and lived alongside Bill in his latter years. He is a great mentor, work associate, and more particularly, an unselfish friend who enjoys sharing his inheritance unconditionally. This generosity makes me wonder what Australia may have been like if we had listened to the wisdom of people like Bill from the point of western colonisation.

In this book, Bill relives the past in order to give some meaningful structure to the future. It is an attempt to help non-Aboriginal people understand the bond between Aboriginal people and their traditionally inherited land. It is for Bill's descendants as well as ours. He knows that every human being has the responsibility of caring for the land. He also knows that in the days to come, many other people will be making decisions for the land he now speaks for.

This is his way of speaking into the future. All of us who read these thoughts will also carry that responsibility.

Kakadu National Park is the scenic, scientific and culturally diverse place it is today because of people like Bill. I hope, like myself, you enjoy some of the unique cultural insight that this book contains.

IAN MORRIS
'Riyala',
Northern Territory
November 2001

BILL NEIDJIE

ARCHAEOLOGICAL WORK in the East Alligator River area evidences a continuous occupation of the region by Aboriginal people for the last 25,000 years. Such work also confirms that pigments for painting were prepared at least 18,000 years ago.

During the glacial period of 20,000 years ago, when the coast was a further 250 kilometres north and the flood plains perhaps 100 metres above the sea level, the Aboriginal people were fresh-water river people occupying the Alligator Rivers areas. With the melting of the glaciers, the sea level rose and the Alligator Rivers environment changed. As the sea approached its present day level, the area became estuarine and Aboriginal people ranged across a landscape – including water lilies and geese – similar to that which we see today.

Aboriginal occupation of the Alligator Rivers area has embraced a time span beyond which most people can conceive. When Moses was leading the exodus from Egypt, Aboriginal occupation of the Alligator Rivers had been continuous for at least 218 centuries. When Christ was embarking on his ministry in Galilee, Aboriginal people had occupied the Alligator Rivers for almost 230 centuries

The arrival of Captain James Cook in Australia had been preceded, then, by over 250 centuries of continuous occupation in the Alligator Rivers. This occupation included what has been identified in recorded history as the estate of the Gagudju (Kakadu) people, and in particular the Bunitj Clan estate of Big Bill Neidjie.

The earliest accounts of European contact with the Gagudju come from the explorer Ludwig Leichhardt. In November and December of 1844, Leichhardt and his party travelled through the area noting that the country was well populated.

> The natives were very numerous and employing themselves either in fishing or burning the grass on the plains, or digging for roots. I saw here a noble fig-tree, under the shade of which seemed to have been the camping place of the natives for the last century.
> (Leichhardt 1847: 493)

The total Aboriginal population of the area at the time of Leichhardt's contact was probably in excess of 2,000 people.

Following European contact, a serious decline in the population took place. In 1922 Paddy Cahill, a well-known buffalo hunter in the region, stated that he would not be able to muster more than a hundred Aborigines in the area.

Census figures for the 1960s confirmed fears that there were few local people alive. A census return for 1965 lists only two Gagudju people as well as Charlie Whittaker (an elderly Aboriginal friend of Bill Neidjie listed as belonging to the 'Gunwinggo' tribe). A 1966 census listed only Bill's close friend Felix Holmes (Iyanuk) of the Limilngan language group and two elderly Gagudju people in the area.
Bill Neidjie is one of the few of the remaining Gagudju.

Big Bill Neidjie was born at Alawanydjawany on the East Alligator River in the mid 1920s or earlier. Bill, like his father Nadampala before him, is of the Bunitj clan (*gunmugurrkurr*), Gagudju language group.

Bill was raised in the East Alligator area. He lived at Ubirr for maybe one year when his mother, Lucy Wirlmaka, was about 21 years old. Here he learnt to hunt and to manage the resources of his environment. His father, his grandfather and his uncles instructed Bill in Gagudju law.

While Bill was still a child his mother stencilled his hand in ochre on a rock shelter at the site known as Walkarr, on the Bunitj clan estate, where it remains today.

Bill's mother, from the Ulbuk clan of the Amurrak language group, took Bill to live at Cape Don 180 kilometres north of East Alligator when Bill was 12 or 13 years of age. He lived there with his mother's family for 5 or 6 years. 'Old Billy Manilugu, we lived with him. He was a buffalo hunter. He knew all the (Aboriginal) law.'

Billy Manilungu was a prominent ceremonial leader throughout the entire region. 'He was a big song man.' Billy Manilugu taught Bill much of the traditional

These photos of the Northern Territory buffalo industry were taken by Ryko when Bill was a small boy. [Northern Territory & Information Service]

Aboriginal law. After the Second World War he particularly taught Bill's friend, Iyanuk (Felix Holmes) of the Limilngan Clan, many of the songs necessary for the continuance of the Morak ceremonial cycle of which Bill and Iyanuk are custodians.

Bill returned to East Alligator intermittently until he was about 20 years of age. At that time Bill's mother took up residence at Cape Don on a permanent basis where she stayed until her mother passed away.

As a young man in company with his friend Toby Gangali of the Mirrarr clan, Bill started work with the buffalo hunters at Cannon Hill but did not stay long. 'Me and Toby, we used to run away from them buffalo hunters. We were too young.'

From about 22 years of age, Bill worked for several years at a timber mill in Mountnorris Bay ('Iwal, that's near Minimini Creek') for Chan Long. Bill then was engaged to cart timber to Darwin in the lugger *Maskee*. The work continued from Mountnorris Bay until the mill at Croker Island took over. Bill worked with the Croker mill for a further three years. 'There was no mission there then. Soon as war came, mission started for coloured people.'

Bill then started work with Leo Hickey on his lugger along the north coast run. On one occasion, Leo Hickey, with Bill in his employ, was engaged to transport 20 to 30 people to the new settlement of Maningrida. But, as Bill relates, the task was not entirely successful. 'They did not stay there because after two weeks there were no smokes (cigarettes) left.'

During the Second World War, Bill returned to the East Alligator area where he lived at Paw Paw Beach (Murgenella Creek). There, an Ubarr ceremony was performed. Participation in an Ubarr ceremony is one of the most important events in a Gagudju man's life. Ruben Cooper, the son by an Aboriginal woman, of one of the first European buffalo hunters, was a senior man overseeing that particular performance of the Ubarr ceremony.

'Ruben Cooper told me to get in that Ubarr. Otherwise it would be too late for me and I would miss it. He said, "In two weeks when you finished that ceremony you come and see me." Two dozen of us young fellers went in (to be initiated into the ceremony).' Bill and fellow initiates were under the control of senior ceremonial leaders. Severe restrictions are placed on initiates who are isolated during the performance of the Ubarr ceremony, including eating and drinking prohibitions. 'Those old men never even let us move. They tell us, "See that big well over there? We'll put you in it and you'll be dead if you disobey." But three men were waiting for us ... with spears. "Where you going?" they say. We were so scared we was shaking all over.'

Some time later, Ruben Cooper became ill. 'There was no medicine so he died. But, half way before he died, he said to me, "I don't know if I'll see you again. You look after the land." Then he died.'

In recent years Bill has again become a permanent resident on his own land. In 1979 Bill was a claimant in the Alligator Rivers Stage II Land Claim heard before Justice Toohey, the Aboriginal Land Commissioner. The Bunitj people of the Gagudju language group were awarded title to their land as a result of this claim.

The identity of an Aboriginal person, however, is much more than legal title to land. He must fulfil the responsibilities with which his people were charged by ancestral beings in the creative epoch.

For Gagudju Man, Big Bill Neidjie, land is life.

1981

Post Script

Ruben, Charlie, Felix, and Toby are gone. Their spirits have gone back to their country. Big Bill is the last of the old Gagudju. But his dream has come true ...... the title to Bunitj land is secure and a new generation of Gagudju is growing up with Gagudju law.

> *I belong to this earth.*
> *Soon my bones become earth ... all the same.*
> *My spirit has gone back to my country ... my mother.*
> *Now my children got to hang onto this story ...*
> *I hang onto this story all my life.*
> *My children can't lose it.*
>
> *This law,*
> *This country,*
> *This people,*
> *All the same ...*
> *Gagudju.*

STEPHEN DAVIS, 2001

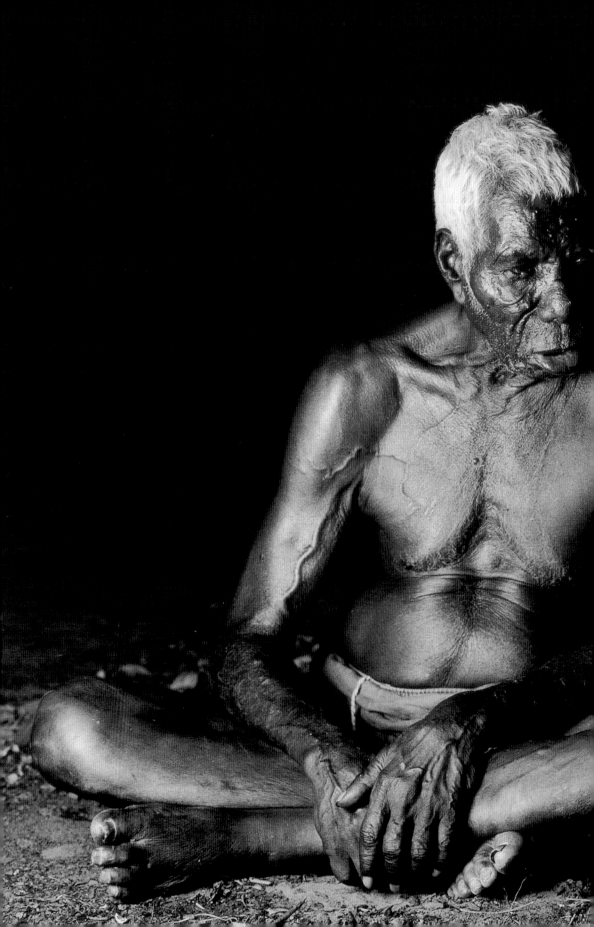

The Words of Bill Neidjie

'I Give You This Story'

I give you this story,
this proper, true story.
People can listen.
I'm telling this while you've got time,
time for you to make something,
you know,
history
book.

I was thinking.
No history written for us
when white European start here,
only few words written.
Should be more than that.

Should be written way Aborigine was live.
That floodplain.
My father, my mother, my grandfather
all used to hunt there, use ironwood spear.
No clothes then.

When I was growing up
good mob of people all around then.
Now people bit wicked.
My time never do little bit wrong,
otherwise get spear straight away.
Now, little bit cheeky mob.
Old time they would all be dead now.
Old people were hard.
I frightened when young.
Only few people now,
But it easy for this mob.

Anyway, got to be made that book.
There's still time.
No man can growl at me for telling this story,
because it will be too late.
I'll be dead.

He can't move his country

This earth
I never damage.
I look after.
Fire is nothing,
just clean up.
When you burn,
new grass coming up.
That mean good animal soon.
Might be goose, long-neck turtle, goanna, possum.
Burn him off,
new grass coming up,
new life all over.

I don't know about white European way.
We, Aborigine, burn.
Make things grow.
Tree grow,
every night he grow.
Daylight
he stop.
Just about dark,
he start again.
Just about morning, I look.
I say, 'Oh, nice tree this.'

When you sleep,
tree growing like other trees,
they got lots of blood.

Rotten tree,
you got to burn him.
Use him to cook.
He's finished up,
cook or roast in coals,
White man cook in oven,
From university that.
Aborigine didn't know that before.
Now all this coming up with Toyota.

First people come to us,
they started and run our life... quick.
They bring drink.
First they should ask about fish, cave, dreaming,
but
they rush in.
They make school. Teach.

Now Aborigine losing it,
losing everything.
Nearly all dead my people,
my old people gone.

Those first people was too quick,
wasn't Aborigine fault.
Still Aborigine all around 1929,
1952, 1953 few left but...
1970 to 1979... gone.
Only me, Robin Gaden and Felix Holmes.

Each man he stay,
stay on his own country.
He can't move his country
so he stay there,
stay with his language.
Language is different,
like skin.
Skin can be different,
but blood same.

Blood and bone,
all same.
Man can't split himself.

White European can't say,
'Oh, that Aborigine no good.'
Might be that Aborigine alright.
Man can't growl at Aborigine,
Aborigine can't growl at white European.
Because both ways.
Might be both good men,
might be both no good.
You never know.

So you should get understand yourself.
No matter Aborigine or white European.

I was keeping this story myself.
It was secret in my mind
but I see what other people doing,
and I was feeling sad.

Law

Law never change,
always stay same.
Maybe it hard,
but proper one for all people.

Not like white European law,
always changing.
If you don't like it,
you can change.

Aboriginal law never change.
Old people tell us,
'You got to keep it.'
It always stays.

Creek, plain, hill.
That plain can change.
Wet season, him mud.
You get lily,
you get fish.
But, he dry up...
that's alright.
Then people can get long-neck turtle.
Same for animal.
People look for food,
animal look for food.
Lizard look,
bird look,
anyone look.
We all same.

Each billabong can be dry...
no fish, turtle, nothing.
He want new water,
then fish and turtle,
make him new one.
New rain coming up,
That rain make everything again.
Plenty fish, turtle, lily.

Rain for us, for anybody.
Rain give us everything new.
Yam, fish, everything.

Barramundi good in the wet season,
still good after the wet because of rain.
Big barramundi from salt water.
He follow fresh water down river,
rain helping him.
He can make eggs.

We must get rain.
Law says we get rain.
He come along wet season
and go dry season.
Rain come down
and give us new fresh water.
Plants coming up new.
Yam, creeper, all plants new.
Then we get fruit, honey and things to live.

Tree, he change with rain.
He get new leaf,
he got to come because rain.
Yam he getting big too.

Old people say
'You dig yam?
Well you digging your granny or mother
through the belly.
You must cover it up,
cover again.
When you get yam you cover over,
then no hole through there.
Yam can grow again.'

'You hang onto this story,' they say.
So I hang on.
I tell kids.
When they get yam, leave hole.
I say
'Who leave that hole?
Cover him up!'
They say
'We forget.'
I tell them
'You leaving hole.
You killing yam.
You killing yourself.
You hang onto your country.
That one I fight for.
I got him.
Now he's yours.
I'll be dead,
I'll be coming to earth.'

All these places for us,
all belong Gagudju.
We use them all the time.
Old people used to move around,
camp different place.
Wet season, dry season,
always camp different place.
Wet season
we camp high place,
get plenty goose egg.
No trouble for fresh water.

Dry season,
move along floodplain
billabong got plenty food.
Even food there when everything dry out.

All Gagudju used to visit,
used to come here to billabong,
dry season camp.
Plenty file snake, long-neck turtle.
Early dry season,
good lily.
Just about middle dry season
file snake, long-neck turtle,
lily flowering.

Everybody camp,
like holiday.
Plenty food this place.
Good time for ceremony,
stay maybe one or two weeks.

Pelican, Jabiru, White Cockatoo,
all got to come back,
make him like before.

Fish,
he listen.
He say,
'Oh, somebody there.'
Him frightened, too many Toyota.
Make me worry too.

I look after my country,
now lily coming back.
Lily, nuts, birds, fish.
Whole lot coming back.

We got to look after,
can't waste anything.
We always used what we got,
old people and me.

If man leave one or two barramundi behind
he go bad.
Trouble,
big fight.
He can't waste anything.
My culture's hard,
but got to be to keep him.
If you waste him anything now,
Next year you can't get as much
because you already waste.

When I was young I never wasted,
otherwise straight away I get trouble.
Even bone not wasted,
Make soup or burn that bone.
Watch out...
That might be dreaming one too.

That story change him now.
It should still be,
but young people won't listen.
Just chuck him away.
Waste him,
destroy everything.

When we young...
my time, Felix's time,
we never eat big fish.
That fish for old people.

Same for goose.
Young people only eat shoulder of goose,
older people must have goose first.
Same for Oenpelli, Mary River, all over.
If young people eat goose or fish,
then he'll be dead.
No young people touch him big fish or goose.
If touch him,
law says got to die.

You know frill-neck lizard?
He look funny.
Used to be good smooth animal.
He was man.
He done something wrong.
Look ugly now... skinny leg, arm,
big one ear, frill-neck.
What he done?
Break law.

He went to sacred ceremony....
called Ubarr.
He didn't listen,
clapping hands.
Old people tell him
'You break law,
you'll be skinny,
you won't grow more.
People will see you like that.'

And he went like that...
big ear.
'You'll be like that for ever and ever.'

Lizard say,
'You make me back like I was before.'
People say 'No,
you break law.
You got to stay like that,
it's law.'

We can't break law.
No, we can't break law.
That frill-neck lizard done it first,
now look how thin he is.
That his own fault.
He spoilt ceremony.

We can't change it.
That's law.

Land

People.
they can't listen for us.
They just listen for money.
Money.

We want goose, we want fish.
Other men want money.
Him can make million dollars,
but only last one year.
Next year him want another million.
Forever and ever him make million dollars.
Him die.

Million no good for us.
We need this earth to live because
we'll be dead,
we'll become earth.

This ground and this earth,
like brother and mother.

Trees and eagle.
You know eagle?
He can listen.
Eagle our brother,
like dingo our brother.

We like this earth to stay,
because he was staying for ever and ever.

We don't want to lose him.
We say 'Sacred, leave him.'

Goanna is dead
because they cutting its body off us,
cutting our mother's belly,
grandpa's bones.
They squash him up.
No good,
And carve up our earth.
No good.

We come from earth, bones.
We go to earth, ashes.

My children got to hang onto this story.
This important story.
I hang onto this story all my life.
My father tell me this story.
My children can't lose it.

White European want to know
asking 'What this story?'
This not easy story.
No-one else can tell it
because this story for Aboriginal culture.

I speak English for you,
so you can listen,
so you can know,
you will understand.
If I put my language in same place,
you won't understand.

Our story is in the land.
It is written in those sacred places.
My children will look after those places,
that's the law.

No-one can walk close to those sacred places.
No difference for Aborigine or white European,
that's the law.
We can't break law.

Old people tell me,
'You got to keep law.'
'What for?' I said.
'No matter we die but that law,
you got to keep it.
No camping in secret place,
no fire there,
no play for kids.
You can't break law.
Law must stay.'

When that law started?
I don't know how many thousands of years.
European say 40,000 years,
but I reckon myself probably was more
because...
it is sacred.

Dreaming place,
you can't change it,
no matter who you are.
No matter you rich man,
no matter you king.
You can't change it.

We say that's secret because dreaming there.
We frightened you might get hurt if you go there,
not only my country but any secret place.
No matter if it Croker Island, Elcho Island,
Brisbane or Sydney.

Wherever, you'll get him same
because that secret place not small.
Secret place is biggest one.
Everywhere.
Powerful.

We walk on earth,
we look after,
like rainbow sitting on top.
But something underneath,
under the ground.
We don't know.
You don't know.

What you want to do?
If you touch,
you might get cyclone, heavy rain or flood.
Not just here,
you might kill someone in another place.
Might be kill him in another country.
You cannot touch him.

These very important places,
but we frightened that European might touch him.
If we tell white European story,
he slow to listen.
If we get little bit wild,
he might listen. But slow.

Him got to always ask question.
He want that place.
That's why we frightened.
I worry about that place.
Secret place.
That got painting there, inside cave.
It got to be looked after because
my father, grandad all look after.
Now me,
I got to do same.
If that painting get rubbed off
there might be big trouble.
That important story.
It for all round this area.
That biggest story,
biggest place.

My grandpa teach me.
That painting is true.
Fish, python, goose,
all painting there.
Grandpa say
'You see painting,
Fish, you got to eat.
Python, you got to eat.
Mullet, you got to eat.
Lily, turtle, all same.
They for you.'

That drawing there, painting,
that's the size fish should be now.
Used to be that size.
I saw them myself.
Used to be that size at Oenpelli
Need two men to carry one catfish.
That was when I was nearly man,
still young.

Now?
Little boy can carry catfish.
Should be fifty pounds,
but only fifteen pounds.

You can't see big fish anymore,
not at Oenpelli.
People say, 'Plenty fish there.
You see barramundi.'

I say
'Yes, pocket fish.'
They say
'What you mean?'
I tell them,
'Pocket fish that barramundi,
little one.
You can put him in your pocket.'

They tell me
'Big catfish,
we got him plenty.'
I say
'Should be ten times size of that.'

We have to keep pressure on young people to learn.
They must learn these things.
I have to stay on to teach my children.
But, young people spread out.
It like that every time we have meetings,
meeting for ceremony.
We make arrangement...
you know... appointment,
about business, secret.
Young people all in town.

You look now...
Nobody with me.
This old man here (Iyanuk, Felix Holmes)
he with me,
but we don't have a dozen behind us.
So, we must stay on.
Look after and teach.

All my uncle gone,
but this story I got him.
They told me.
They taught me
and I can feel it.

I feel it with my body,
with my blood.
Feeling all these trees,
all this country.
When this wind blow you can feel it.
Same for country,
You feel it.
You can look.
But feeling...
that make you.

Feeling make you.
Out there in open space,
he coming through your body.
Look while he blow and feel with your body,
because tree just about your brother or father
and tree is watching you.

Earth.
Like your father or brother or mother,
because you born from earth.
You got to come back to earth.
When you dead,
you'll come back to earth.
Maybe little while yet...
then you'll come to earth.
That's your bone, your blood.
It's in this earth,
same as for tree.

Tree.
He watching you.
You look at tree,
he listen to you.
He got no finger,
he can't speak.

But that leaf,
he pumping, growing,
growing in the night.

While you sleeping
you dream something.
Tree and grass same thing.
They grow with your body,
with your feeling.

If you feel sore,
headache, sore body,
that mean somebody killing tree or grass.

You feel
because your body in that tree or earth.
Nobody can tell you,
you got to feel it yourself.

Tree might be sick,
you feel it.
You might feel it for two or three years.
You get weak,
little bit, little bit.
Because tree going bit by bit.
Dying.

Tree not die when you cut it.
He not die tomorrow, he still green.
Might be five or six weeks,
might be two months.
You feel it then.

Your body.
You feel it.

Environment

Those trees,
they grow and grow.
Every night they grow.
That grass,
no matter it burn.
When it drink,
it grow again.
When you cut tree,
it pump life away,
all the same as blood in my arm.

Earth,
same thing.
You brought up with earth, tree, water.

Water is your blood.
Water,
you can't go without water.
No matter no food two days,
three day, four day,
if you got water.
If no water,
little bit weak,
getting hard.
Water important.

That's why we get story.
Old people tell us about that first lightning.
That's before wet season.
We can't look at it.
Later we get lightning and rain from other way.
But, must not look at first lightning,
bend head down
like first woman who looked.
She was ashamed and bent her head.
We must do the same.

Sky,
cloud.
Made for us.
Star,
he'll stay for ever and ever.

When you lying down in the night,
look at star.

I was lying down,
I look star.
It make me remember when I was young.

When young I think that star really river,
river and creek.
You call it Southern Cross,
that other star.
We say it spear and crocodile.

So, I just look.
I remember other star,
eagle,
eagle on other side.

I look at star.
I know just about time for wet season,
may be time for dry season.
I know from star.

Well now that star over here,
so look out for wet season.
That star right down in December.
When that wet season come,
that star come back.
I say, 'Well, dry season coming.'
Then rain finish him up.

October
up high.
November
getting low.
December
right down.

My grandpa taught me that.
He said,
'Don't forget this.
Tell this story with kids
so he can listen
slow.

And then story will come for him,
exactly like this.
This story right, exactly right,
because it dreaming.'

Death

We all lying down on grass in dry season.
Look up at stars.
I tell kids,
'See them stars.
They been there million years.
They always be there.'

I see pink star.
I tell them 'That King Brown Snake.'
I see his eye,
that pink one.
That star he work.
He go pink, white, pink, white.
That King Brown he look at night.

Eagle, star,
we got him story.
What you call him?
Mars that one,
really eagle.
One arm short,
left wing long one.
His wing been burnt.

Three or four kind of eagle here.
Proper one really that black one.
He can kill him black wallaby.
Proper eagle that one.
Other one with white chest,
he can go billabong or salt water.
But, black one proper eagle.

I look at moon.
It tell me story, like stars.
Moon,
moon is man.
He said,
'These people will die,
but they'll come back
like I do.
They'll come back to be earth again.'

Native Cat said 'No,
they will be dead and never come back.'
Everyone jump on him and kill him.
They burn him so he got plenty spots.
Spots from hot coals.

So moon say again
'Man will come back,
like I come back each time.
He'll come back to earth.'

I know I come back to my country.
When I die I become earth.
I love this country and this earth.

This story for all people.
Everybody should be listening.
Same story for everyone,
just different language.

My meaning might be little bit hard,
so I speak English.
You just listen careful...
slow.

We got to hang on
not to lose our story.
Don't think about money too much.
You can get million dollar,
but not worth it.
Million dollar,
he just go 'poof'.
Couple of weeks,
you got nothing.

This ground never move.
I'll be buried here.
I'll be with my brother, my mother.
If I lose this,
where I'll be buried?
I'm hanging onto this ground.
I'll become earth again.
I belong to this earth.
And earth should stay with us.

Tree the same as me.
When he get old he'll die.
He'll be dead and burn.
He'll leave his ashes behind.
Tree become earth.

When I die,
I become skeleton.
I'll be in cave.
That way my spirit stay there.

I seen new coffin three or four times.
No good.
I don't want coffin,
just cave.

Should be keep our law.

Coffin no good for Aborigine,
got to put bones back where they belong.
Man die.
Soon as him ready,
pick him up,
take him.
Take him to cave.
His shadow,
his spirit,
will stay with him.

If you go in cave
you must call out.
If you've got young man with you,
he might be stranger for that cave,
for that spirit.

You got to call out first.
You must signal,
must sing out
because old people used to tell us,
'Your father,
your grandad,
your aunty,
they'll be waiting for you.
Call out,
they'll listen.
They'll know you,
and they say,
That stranger
we can't hurt him.'

Old people tell me,
'When you dead you'll be buried.
Uncle bury you in sacred place.'

They told me,
'Don't be rough in your life.
If you too rough,
little bit mistake.'
I said 'What mistake?
No-one can kill me with spear.'
They say
'Yes, we know,
nobody kill you on outside.'

'No mark in your body.
But inside,
when you feeling sick,
sick in your body.
Headache is nothing.
But in your body,
get very bad sick.'
I ask, 'Why?'
They say,
'See that big tree?'
I said
'Yes, I chop him down that tree.
I play,
I cut him.'

'You cut yourself,' they say.
'When you maybe forty years,
might be fifty years old,
you feel pain in your back,
because you cut tree.
I'm old man,' he said,
I'm telling you.'

Land got to stay,
always stay same.
No matter little track,
grass still grow,
bush can grow.

But soon as bitumen there,
all finished.

Grass don't grow,
Maybe little bit side,
but middle... nothing.
You look where timber
gone,
pulled out.
Bulldozer rip it out.

Well, you feel it in your body.
You say,
'That tree same as me.'
This piece of ground he grow you.

Conclusion

Rock stays,
earth stays.

I die and put my bones in cave or earth.
Soon my bones become earth,
all the same.

My spirit has gone back to my country,
my mother.

This story is important.
It won't change,
it is law.
It is like this earth,
it won't move.

Ground and rock,
he can't move.
Cave,
he never move.
No-one can shift that cave,
because it dream.
It story.
It law.

This law,
this country,
this people,
No matter what people,
red, yellow, black or white,
the blood is the same.
Lingo little bit different,
but no matter.
Country,
you in other place.
But same feeling.
Blood, bone,
all the same.

This story,
this is true story.

My people
all dead.
We only got few left.
That's all, not many.
We getting too old.

Young people.
I don't know if they can hang onto this story.

But, now you know this story,
and you'll be coming to earth.
You'll be part of earth when you die.
You responsible now.
You got to go with us.
To earth.
Might be you can hang on.
Hang onto this story.
To this earth.

You got children,
grandson.
Might be your grandson will get this story,
keep going,
hang on like I done.

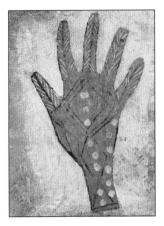

THE BEGINNING

THE OCCUPATION OF AUSTRALIA by humans probably began as long ago as 65,000 years when, during a period of low sea level, a small group of coastal people made a remarkable ocean voyage across the final gap separating this land from the Indonesian lowlands. Noone will ever know what drove these people on. It may have been population pressure which was the direct cause now that the vast inter-island Sunda plains had been exposed by the retreating sea of an ice age. Or was it the seasonal drift of smoke from fires burning in the greatly increased area of woodlands from over the south-eastern horizon, which lured them on? Did the steady north-west monsoon which, along with bamboo, and other flotsam – including people on flimsy rafts – simply drive them here, like it drove the later Maccassans, Vietnamese and the boat people from Middle East.

Whatever the reason, these were people of the coasts, people who lived by the sea and with the sea. Once they had conquered the problem of flotation, their arrival was inevitable. They arrived, not as an invading force and not as purposeful colonists, but as 'lost' people saved when they beached on the long low mangrove-covered shores of north-western Australia. Whatever their mode of arrival, they came long, long ago, perhaps two thousand generations before the pyramids were built.

Eight generations ago, Cook's belated 'discoveries' set in motion the forces which have all but destroyed this Aboriginal culture, a culture rooted in 65,000 years experience of the Australian environment.

A vision of the richness and depth of that experience comes through in Big Bill Neidjie's wisdom. But we get ahead of our story.

It is most likely that the Ancestor Aboriginals arrived at a time when a glacial period was in full swing. The sea level had dropped some 100 metres. The last time the levels were as low as that was between 15,000 and 20,000 years ago. However, at that time people were grinding their tools near the caverns by the East Alligator (a world first in technology), and Aborigines had been camping by Lake Mungo for at least 30,00 and more years. The low sea level previous to the last was between 50,000 and 55,000 years ago. That then is a likely arrival period.

Even with these low sea levels the trip to Australia required a substantial voyage of up to ninety kilometres, perhaps making the Ancestors the first mariners. They landed on a combined North Australian New Guinean coast which was then seawards 300-500 kilometres north-west of the present coast.

The beach and what lay ahead was a vast unknown plain in the minds of these very early navigators. The oceanic gap separated the Australian realm from the Asian. Tigers and leopards gave way to thylacines and marsupial lions; buffalo, rhinoceros and pigs to diprotodons, kangaroos, and wallabies; monkeys to koalas, possums and phalangers. Now two worlds had drifted close enough for humans to enter and be nonplussed by the old Australian creatures. Some northern animals, the rodents and bats for instance, had made it earlier while some other animals – the crocodiles and turtles for example – were common to both worlds.

But like Neil Armstrong or Columbus, those first settlers must have found Australia and New Guinea a new and mysterious place.

The first people were navigators with a tradition of food, shelter and understandings which were coastal. As the Ancestors moved about the land, they saw, remembered and explained the features. So far as humans were concerned, their discoveries created a 'new' landscape, just as Columbus had 'created' the Americas for Spaniards.

As a child builds up a perception of place through accumulated experience, so too did these early generations accumulate perceptions of landscape – of their habitat. Place was associated with natural phenomena, in particular, powerful elements such as lightning, floods, fire and volcanoes. Over time, this growing net of perceptions were given authority and coherence and effectively passed on from generation to generation by being linked with, creation heroes. The environment and humans were gradually being seen as parts of the same processes of the living world.

Bird, he gone now. He was talking. He gone.
He say goodnight, he go sleep might be.

All kind of animal come to you because that mean you
got story, and they know your story.
That not really bird, but spirit, spirit of these people.
They were camping here, and they watching us,
to look after us, might be.

Good for them, and good for you.

Make you good.

Good feeling.

Over the generations, traditions of the people became increasingly complex. These traditions were woven into the structure of society, into the relationships between people, and between people and their habitat. Accumulated experience became so great that even the oldest individual could not retain it all. Without a written language this wisdom of the people remained in many living minds. These minds were living in a landscape every part of which was a permanent reminder of perception and explanation. This information was passed on from generation to generation. So it is that the modern Aboriginal person inherits a culture where landscape is critical to maintaining physical, mental and spiritual life. Key parts of the landscape are referred to as 'sacred sites' – but does the word 'sacred' have the depth of meaning that can convey the values attached to these places?

So, through 50,000 or more years, the environment which sustained life and culture, became bound intimately with every aspect of human life. Aboriginal and environment were one and the same. Ownership of land in the European sense did not exist: Aboriginal people were part of the living systems. Through their mythology they understood that their Ancestors created the landscape and the life on it. This life included themselves, with each person playing a role in the maintenance of the whole dynamic world: this was key to the maintenance of their community and to their continued survival.

The most important role that an individual human could play in this system was that of custodian of the common environment. First chairman of the Northern LandCouncil, Silas Roberts, put it this way:

> *Aboriginals have a special connection with everything that is natural. Aboriginals see themselves as part of nature. We see all things natural as part of us. All the things on Earth we see as part-human. This is told through the idea of dreaming. By dreaming we mean the belief that long ago these creatures started human society.*

> *These creatures, these great creatures, are just as much alive today as they were in the beginning. They are everlasting and will never die. They are always part of the land and nature as we are. Our connection to all things natural is spiritual.*

Stephen Davis, while teaching at Milingimbi, Arnhem Land, made many offshore fishing trips with local Aboriginal people. He soon became aware that his hosts avoided some areas of water and consistently turned back when the boat drifted across seemingly imaginary lines. When asked for an explanation, the people shrugged and said that the place was someone else's land. Triangulating features

All Gagudju used to visit,
used to come here to billabong,
dry season camp.

Plenty file snake, long-neck turtle.
Early dry season,
good lily.

Just about middle dry season
file snake, long-neck turtle,
lily flowering.

Everybody camp,
like holiday.

Plenty food this place.
Good time for ceremony,
stay maybe one or two weeks.

Pelican, Jabiru, White Cockatoo,
all got to come back,
make him like before.

Top above: Magpie Goose.
Left: bush berries (rich in Vitamin C).
Above: the long necked turtle.

along the coast from the boat, Davis found that these places of turnaround were indeed consistent. Davis made many miles of soundings along the north coast and around Bathurst and Melville Islands. In each instance he found that the 'imaginary' lines actually follow undersea ridges and valley bottoms. His findings showed that, accurately bound into traditional behaviour, is knowledge of ice-age geography, of a landscape that disappeared five thousand years before the birth of Christ. To this day, some places under 30 metres of water are maintained as cased sites. To coastal people, land and water are one and the same. Tradition has it that, although the sea has had them in retreat, one day they will return to their submerged land.

With rising sea levels following melting of the ice, the meandering lower reaches of the Alligator Rivers became tidal estuaries. Mud built up along banks, cutting off side backswamps and mudflats. Sands were swept by wave, current and tide into bars and spits – building beach ridges between points, cutting off the sea and forming lagoon systems. Each bar, ridge and lagoon formed new zones for life. The mangroves moved in, becoming the habitat for more than twenty species, along with the animal components of these rich nurseries of marine life.

Geography and seasonality ruled the Aboriginal lives through their effect on access and food supply. This occured, not so much by controlling the supply of food, but by maintaining the variety as seasonal changes ushered in new foods. The Aboriginal seasonal calendar, based on six seasons, emphasises this point and today is increasingly acknowledged and worked with by land managers in the Top End of the Northern Territory. To indicate the complex ecological understandings which have developed, I quote from the Arnhem Land Environ Series published by the Milingimbi Literature Production Centre, Book 4, **Rrarranhdharr.**

> *We know that Dharratharramirri (season) is coming to an end when balgurr (Brachychiton paradoxis) starts to lose its leaves. At the same time the pandanus (Gunga: Pandanusyirrkalensis) starts to fruit and Dhimurru (East- South -East) wind blows. The really cold mornings and mists are nearly gone. Sharks are giving birth to their young. They are called burrugu and so we call this season Burrugumirri. This is a very short season which only lasts for a few weeks. Stingrays are also called burrugu at this time. If munydjutj (Buchanania obovata) is flowering, then we are really sure that they are fat.*

How fascinating it is to see the flowering of a plant as an indicator of stingrays being fat! How much experience and memory was needed to distil that relationship. This deeply integrated view of the human environment rests on the fact that the Aboriginal landscape has become fully personalised.

But how is such a store of tradition passed on, particularly without a written language? It happens primarily because life and learning are synonymous. Even a cursory look at the Bunitj year will illustrate the point. Tradition is continuously demonstrated and practised as a staged learning process, culminating at its richest point at the moment of death. Transmission is by way of myth, stories, field experiences, play, song cycles, dances, the pattern and design of artefacts along with the ritual of ceremonies.

The form of the area and its biota is seen to reflect the activities of the Ancestors. In the beginning, the Bunitj land, Bill Neidjie's land, was a blank plain. An Ancestral Being, Indjuwanydjuwa, travelled this landscape. His daily activities of hunting, gathering food and performing rituals, gave form to the landscape. He lived in a rock shelter on the wall on which was a painting depicting him. Following his acts of creation he turned himself into a great stone standing in a billabong surrounded by a sea of pink lotus lilies.

Today on Bunitj land, a chain of sites of varying importance defines the route of Indjuwanydjuwa's travels. The maintenance of these sites, along with their stories, rituals and songs, is the responsibility of the senior man of the clan.

A number of Ancestral Beings may have been involved in the creation of the landscape and its biota, including the humans. Some of these Beings were female, one of whom was involved in the birth of the Bunitj language group.

Some of the movements of other Ancestors took them into and across lands occupied by adjoining clans and therefore the stories and ceremonies related to these movements are shared and jointly enacted.

The coastal lowlands of the East Alligator River have been exposed by the retreating sandstone Arnhem Land Plateau. At lower sea levels the river cuts broad valleys in the ancient basement rocks. In places, isolated outliers of sandstone rise like islands from the lowland ridges. Subsequently the broad valleys fill with mud and became swampy plains. During wet seasons these plains become a vast wetland and as much as half of the Bunitj land goes under water.

Four distinct food producing zones are used at varying times according to the seasons: black soil floodplain, the stone country of the outliers and plateau, monsoon forest and eucalypt woodland forests. Before the coming of non-Aboriginals probably 40 to 60 people lived on this area, a number augmented from time to time by visits from adjoining clans. Some camps, as at Ubirr, were regularly used by eight clans, but always after permission had been sought from the traditional owner.

Movement was initiated by changes in food supply and the seasons, attendance at ceremonies and the need to be comfortable in this harsh environment. A man walking alone would cover 15 to 30 kilometres a day while a family with children would travel 8 to 10 kilometres between camps. Some traditional walks which linked people into a sequence of ceremonial activities and renewal of relationships with country, were of considerable magnitude– the Badmardi Clan of Kakadu had a recorded two month marathon of some 600 kilometres.

One could write much more about the depth of knowledge these people have about the natural community to which they and we belong. They are continually learning the processes of living – the landscape itself is not only teacher but textbook as well. In every physical and metaphysical way the Aboriginal people are inextricably bound to their land. These ecosystems were also, to varying degrees, artefacts of the relationship between land and humans, the use of fire as a tool being an obvious example of this process.

I can find no adequate word in English to describe the personalisation of the landscape by Aboriginals. It is little wonder then, that when Europeans arrived, had no capacity to understand these people. These new arrivals did not look for harmonious relationships and complex community structures which created relationships more akin to membership. Instead they looked for evidence of ownership, of manipulation, of control. Many still do.

The words of Big Bill Neidjie are an attempt by an old Aboriginal custodian to pass on to all people some of the wisdom accumulated from the experience of 2000 or more generations. I have known Bill now for 25 years. It has been his greatest concern that his own children and others will 'hang onto' this knowledge, this wisdom.

Bill is on about attitudes and values. The future rests on ours.

ALLAN FOX

Rock stays,
earth stays.

I die and put my bones in cave or earth.
Soon my bones become earth,
all the same.

My spirit has gone back to my country,
my mother.

Dreaming place,
you can't change it,
no matter who you are.
No matter you rich man,
no matter you king.
You can't change it.

I feel it with my body,
with my blood.
Feeling all these trees,
all this country.
When this wind blow you can feel it.
Same for country,
You feel it.
You can look.
But feeling...
that make you.

Feeling make you.
Out there in open space,
he coming through your body.
Look while he blow and feel with your body,
because tree just about your brother or father
and tree is watching you.

Rotten tree.
You got to burn him.
Use him to cook,
He's finished up.
Cook or roast in coals.
White European cook in oven,
from university that.
Aborigine didn't know that before.
Now all this coming up with Toyota.

This earth
I never damage.
I look after.
Fire is nothing,
just clean up.
When you burn,
new grass coming up.

Barramundi good in the wet season,
still good after the wet because of rain.
Big barramundi from salt water.
He follow fresh water down river,
rain helping him.
He can make eggs.

We must get rain.
Law says we get rain.
He come along wet season
and go dry season.
Rain come down
and give us new fresh water.
Plants coming up new.
Yam, creeper. All plants new.
Then we get fruit, honey and things to live.

Tree, he change with rain.
He get new leaf,
he got to come because rain.

Yam he getting big too.

Tree.
He watching you.
You look at tree,
he listen to you.
He got no finger,
he can't speak.
But that leaf
he pumping, growing,
growing in the night.

While you sleeping
you dream something.
Tree and grass same thing.
They grow with your body,
with your feeling.

This ground never move.
I'll be buried here.
I'll be with my brother, my mother.
If I lose this,
where I'll be buried?
I'm hanging onto this ground.
I'll become earth again.
I belong to this earth.
And earth should stay with us.

Tree the same as me.
When he get old he'll die.
He'll be dead and burn.
He'll leave his ashes behind.
Tree become earth.